THE CHESTNUT COOKBOOK

THE CHESTNUT
COOKBOOK

hamlyn

Contents

Introduction 6

Soups and Appetizers 12

Side Dishes and Stuffings 20

Main Courses 26

Sweet Treats 40

Desserts 48

Jams and Chutneys 61

Index 64

First published in 2000
by Hamlyn
an imprint of Octopus Publishing Group Limited
2–4 Heron Quays, London E14 4JP

ISBN 0 600 60226 5

Printed in China

Photographer: Ian Wallace
Home Economist: Dagmar Vesely

Notes

1 The American Egg Board advises that eggs should not be consumed raw. This book contains some dishes made with raw or slightly cooked eggs. It is prudent for more vulnerable people such as pregnant and nursing mothers, invalids, the elderly, babies, and young children to avoid uncooked or lightly cooked dishes made with eggs.

2 Meat and poultry should be cooked thoroughly. To test if poultry is cooked, pierce the flesh through the thickest part with a skewer or fork—the juices should run clear, never pink or red. Keep refrigerated until ready for cooking.

3 This book includes dishes made with nuts and nut derivatives. It is advisable for those with known allergic reactions to nuts and nut derivatives and those who may be potentially vulnerable to these allergies, such as pregnant and nursing mothers, invalids, the elderly, babies, and young children to avoid dishes made with nuts and nut oils. It is also prudent to check the labels of prepared ingredients for the possible inclusion of nut derivatives.

THE CHESTNUT COOKBOOK

Roasted on an open fire, made into a hearty soup, or candied and served with cream, chestnuts are a sure sign of winter warmth. Their sweet, nutty flavor and moist, crumbly texture make them suitable for a whole host of sweet and savory dishes, from soups, stews, and stuffings to soufflés, ice creams, and cakes. And because they contain more starch and less oil than other nuts, they are often served as an accompaniment to traditional turkey at Thanksgiving and other winter holidays. Since prehistoric times, these easily-gathered nutritious nuts have been greatly valued as a food source. Chestnut sellers are a familiar sight on chilly street corners in New York, London, and Paris, huddled over their hot coals, but there is so much more to these delicious nuts, and this book sets out to prove it.

Chestnuts in Europe

Chestnuts have a long history of cultivation in Europe. They are indigenous to southwest Asia, but were brought to southern Europe by the Greeks and to Britain by the Romans.

In fact, their Latin name, *Castanea sativa*, derives from the town of Castanis in Thessaly, where chestnut trees used to grow in abundance. During Roman times, chestnuts formed the basis of a vital economy around the Mediterranean region and the rural and mountainous areas of southern Europe, including the Apennines mountains, Savoy, Sicily, Madeira, and the south of France. Here the poorer people largely subsisted on chestnuts, grinding them to make bread, porridge and stews. So much so that certain areas of the Italian and Swiss Alps were known as the "chestnut civilization" and chestnut trees were referred to as "bread trees".

But chestnuts have not only been valued by the poor. According to Xenophon, members of the Persian nobility were fattened on chestnuts, while coffee houses in many Italian cities served pâtés and cakes made from chestnuts.

So prolific and popular were chestnuts that even the flowers were not neglected. According to John Evelyn, in Corsica, "They also made Fritters of Chestnut-flower which they wet with Rosewater, and sprinkled with grated Parmigiano, and so fry them in fresh Butter, a delicate."

As well as using chestnuts to make bread, they have been traditionally served as sweetmeats in Europe. *Marrons glacés* (candied chestnuts) were created during the reign of Louis XIV and today are a speciality of Privas in the Ardèche, and Italy. They were formerly sold steeped in the syrup in which they were prepared, but now they are more often sold dry with a sugar glaze. One Privas firm has been making chestnut cream (*crème de marron*) since 1882. This is a sweet paste made from chestnut purée, sugar, glucose, and vanilla.

Up to the Present Day

Chestnuts and chestnut flour are still used as a basic food source in some of the more rural areas of Europe. During World War II, chestnut flour is widely credited with sustaining virtually the whole of the Corsican population.

In Corsica there is an annual chestnut hunt called a *séchoir*. The majority of the chestnuts are dried and ground to make flour. Chestnut flour is rather heavy, so is generally mixed *moitié moitié*, half and half, with ordinary flour to lighten the mixture and allow it to rise. The flour is used to make *brilloli*, a chestnut polenta, *castagnacci*, chestnut cake, and many pastries.

In the Ardèche, chestnuts are used to make a speciality salad, and in the Cévennes and southwestern France, they are used in soups, porridges, and jams. In the Valais, on the other hand, *brisolée* is an ancient dish of chestnuts roasted with cheese. All over France and Italy, chestnuts are used in sweet dishes, including Bavarian creams, ice creams, and as a filling for gâteaux roulés, barquettes, and meringues.

There are now many cultivated forms of the chestnut tree in Europe, including hundreds of different varieties. They have been bred to enhance a range of different characteristics which make them particularly suitable for roasting, candying, drying or making flour.

Chestnuts in America

For hundreds of years, chestnut trees flourished over much of the United States, inspiring Henry Thoreau to write of "boundless chestnut woods". A traditional saying stated that so numerous were they in eastern forests, that a squirrel could jump from chestnut tree to chestnut tree all the way from Georgia to New York without touching the ground. The native Americans relied on chestnuts as a dietary staple, and they have provided a nutritious food source for early settlers and generations of Americans since, from Maine to Florida.

The nuts weren't the only thing used. During colonization, the native tree provided the settlers with straight-grained, rot-resistant wood to make railroad ties, house frames, barns, fences, furniture, and fuel. Chestnut trees were an important source of tannin for leather processing as well.

In 1904, however, disaster struck. Chinese chestnut trees that were being imported into the US were found to be carrying a virulent bark fungus. This fungus spread to the native population and killed almost every chestnut tree in the east and mideast in just 40 years. It is estimated that billions of trees died between the Atlantic seaboard and the Mississippi river. It was a catastrophe not only for people who relied on these trees for their livelihood as thousands of jobs were lost, but also for the animals and other wildlife that tried to survive in the now bare forests. Recently, however, a blight-resistant strain has been developed and the American chestnut is making a slow but steady comeback.

Despite the drastic reduction of native trees, chestnuts have remained popular in America and are imported from Europe, particularly Italy, France, and Switzerland. Chestnuts often form part of the traditional Thanksgiving meal, as a delicious addition to the stuffing for the turkey or served with a vegetable such as Brussels sprouts or cabbage. And everyone knows of chestnuts roasting over an open fire around Christmas—they even feature in one of the most popular holiday carols.

Chestnuts and Health

Unlike most nuts that are high in fat and low in starch, chestnuts are in fact very healthy and can form a valuable and nutritious part of anyone's diet. They have a similar nutritional content to wheat or brown rice, containing less than 3 per cent fat (compared to 50 per cent for other nuts), and have a high carbohydrate content of around 40 percent. This makes them energy rich, yielding 200–300 calories per 3½ oz, depending on the variety.

They also contain 5–10 per cent of high-quality protein and are a good source of potassium. Other nutrients found in chestnuts include calcium, iron, sodium, vitamins B1, B2, and vitamin C. They contain no cholesterol.

Buying Chestnuts

Chestnuts are round, heavy, white-fleshed nuts with a thin brown skin and a glossy, brittle brown shell. They are the fruits of the sweet chestnut tree and are not related to either the horse chestnut nor the water chestnut used in Oriental cuisine. The edible part forms inside a spiky outer husk which usually contains three nuts. However, improved cultivated varieties (called *marron* in France) contain a single large nut. These have been bred to make commercial production easier.

Fresh Chestnuts

Fresh chestnuts are available from late September to early February. They should feel heavy and hard, with shiny, blemish-free shells. Nuts with air pockets will feel lighter and are likely to be older and dried out. Some chestnuts can appear to be fresh on the outside but will be spoiled inside, so always buy or collect a few more nuts than you need. Chestnuts can also be bought in the following forms, which are useful when fresh nuts are out of season.

Preserved Chestnuts

Canned: Chestnuts are readily available in cans, usually packed in water. They are ready-peeled and cooked and are very convenient to use.

Vacuum packed: These are similar to canned nuts, but come vacuum-packed in glass jars or in plastic, sometimes with water around them.

Dried: Dried chestnuts can often be found in Italian and Chinese stores. Before use they must be soaked in water to rehydrate them. To reconstitute dried chestnuts, soak overnight (or at least 8 hours) before using. Once soaked, dried chestnuts expand to about twice their original size so, ¼ cup dried chestnuts yields 1½ cups soaked. Before using, remove any of the dark inner skin lodged in the crevices of the soaked chestnuts. A pound of fresh unpeeled chestnuts is equivalent to 1½ cups of soaked dried chestnuts.

Chestnut purée (*purée de marrons*): unsweetened chestnut purée is sold in cans, mainly imported from France or Switzerland.

Chestnut cream (*crème de marrons*): sweetened chestnut purée is available in cans and tubes. It is a speciality of France, from where it is exported all over the world.

Chestnut flour: This is sometimes available in health food stores or Italian delicatessens. If you cannot find any, make your own (see page 10).

Marrons glacés: These are chestnuts that have been poached in syrup for 48 hours and glazed to give them a shiny outer coating. They are eaten alone or used to decorate cakes.

Storage

Fresh chestnuts do not keep well at room temperature, but they will last up to a week in a cool place. Alternatively, place them in a plastic bag, make a few holes in it and store in the refrigerator for up to two weeks.

Whole peeled nuts can be blanched in boiling water and frozen. They will last in good condition for up to one month.

Unused chestnut purée or canned candied chestnuts can be kept in the refrigerator for up to several months. Store covered in an airtight plastic box.

Dried chestnuts can be stored in an airtight container in a cool place for up to two months. They last indefinitely if stored in a refrigerator or freezer. Chestnut flour will last for up to one month in a refrigerator or freezer.

Cooking with Chestnuts

Their sweet, rich taste makes chestnuts suitable for both sweet and savory dishes. They can be served like a vegetable or used in stews or casseroles. Chestnut flour can be used to make dense, flavorsome cakes; chestnut cream can be used as a smooth, scrumptious filling for tarts, meringues, and cakes; and marrons glacés can be crumbled into ice creams or used to decorate puddings.

Peeling Chestnuts

The thin, inner skin must be removed before the chestnut is eaten, as it is very bitter. To do this, use a sharp knife to cut a cross right through the outer shell on the flat side of each nut. Place the nuts in a saucepan, cover with cold water and bring quickly to the boil over a high heat. Boil for one minute, then remove the pan from the heat. Remove the nuts from the hot water one at a time and peel away the shell and inner skin. Chestnuts are easier to peel when they are still hot. Any nut that resists peeling can be returned to the hot water for a few minutes longer. Alternatively, cut through the shells in the same way, then put the nuts in a baking pan with a little water. Roast in a hot oven for about 8 minutes. Some people suggest that the nuts should be shelled when raw, then boiled for 20 minutes in lightly salted water. Then inner skins can then be removed simply.

Boiled Chestnuts

Place some peeled chestnuts in a saucepan and cover with cold water. Season with salt and pepper and add a little chopped celery to the pan. Bring to the boil and simmer gently for 35–45 minutes. Drain well and serve with butter, sprinkled with a little cayenne pepper. Boiled chestnuts make a good accompaniment to plain roast meats such as lamb or turkey. They are also delicious when served with piquant dishes, such as rich meats cooked with citrus fruits.

Chestnut Purée

Boil some peeled chestnuts (see above), drain well and rub through a sieve or food mill. Return to the saucepan with ⅔ cup of cream per 2 pounds of chestnuts. Reheat gently, stirring constantly. Then add 2 ounces of butter per 2 pounds of chestnuts and adjust the seasoning to taste. If the purée is too thick, add a little water or stock.

Braised Chestnuts

Peel the chestnuts and spread them over the base of a large, greased ovenproof casserole dish. Place a bouquet garni and a stick of celery among the nuts, season and add just enough chicken or vegetable stock to cover. Cover the casserole and cook in a hot oven at 425°F for about 45 minutes. Do not stir during cooking or the nuts will break up.

Roasted Chestnuts

See page 16.

Chestnut Flour

Collect the chestnuts as soon as they have fallen, and store in a warm dry room for about six weeks. When thoroughly dry, peel and grind them to as fine a flour as possible, using a flour mill or large pestle and mortar. This is a rather laborious task, but it is worthwhile as chestnut flour imparts an interesting flavor to cakes and breads. The flour will be yellow in color and rather sweet. Mix it half and half with all-purpose flour to lighten it and allow the bread or cake to rise.

Basic Chestnut Preserve

Peel a good quantity of chestnuts, cover with cold water in a saucepan, bring to the boil and cook for 40 minutes. Drain well and rub through a sieve or food mill. Weigh the purée and add an equal weight of sugar. Place in a preserving pan with 6 tablespoons of water per 2 pounds of purée, plus 1–2 vanilla beans. Heat gently, stirring well. The preserve is ready when it comes away from the bottom of the pan when stirred. Remove the vanilla and pour the preserve into sterilized jars.

Hints and Tips

Warm some cooked, peeled chestnuts through in a little butter and use as a garnish for winter soups.

Purée roasted chestnuts with chicken stock to make a sweet, nutty sauce for chicken or turkey.

Crumble roasted or boiled chestnuts on top of a salad.

Add cooked whole or halved chestnuts to stir-fries where they will provide a nutty flavor and starchy bulk.

Chestnuts are often served with Brussels sprouts or red cabbage, but are also delicious with green beans and snap peas.

Prepared chestnuts are great convenience foods—ready-peeled and cooked. Add some to stews, risottos or soups.

CREAM OF CHESTNUT SOUP

I pound chestnuts
I tablespoon oil
¼ pound Canadian bacon, diced
I large onion, chopped
2 celery stalks, chopped
2 carrots, chopped
I bouquet garni
5 cups chicken stock
salt and white pepper

To garnish:
crumbled, cooked bacon
chopped parsley

1 Peel the chestnuts according to the directions on page 9.
2 Heat the oil in a large pot. Add the bacon and onion, and fry for 2 minutes without browning. Next, add the celery, carrots, and bouquet garni, and give a stir. Pour in the stock and season to taste with salt and pepper. Add the peeled chestnuts and bring to a boil. Cover and simmer for 1 hour, or until the chestnuts are soft. Discard the bouquet garni and allow to cool slightly.
3 Purée the soup in a food processor or blender until smooth, or put through a food mill. Return to the pot and reheat.
4 Ladle into bowls, garnish with the crumbled bacon and parsley, and serve hot.

Serves 8
Preparation time: 20 minutes, plus peeling the chestnuts
Cooking time: about 1¼ hours

CHESTNUT AND APPLE SOUP

I pound chestnuts
I tablespoon corn oil
I onion, finely chopped
3 cups chicken stock
1¼ cups dry (alcoholic) cider, or ¾ cup sweet cider plus ½ cup dry white wine
½ pound cooking apples, peeled, cored, and sliced
salt and black pepper

To garnish:
flat-leaf parsley

1 Peel the chestnuts according to the directions on page 9.
2 Put the peeled chestnuts in a clean pot, add water to cover, and bring to a boil. Simmer for 20 minutes, then set aside. Do not drain but reserve to go into the soup.
3 In another large pot, heat the oil. Add the onion, and cook until soft. Then add the stock, cider, apples, chestnuts, and their cooking liquid, and stir to mix. Bring to a boil, then reduce the heat, cover, and simmer for about 15 minutes, or until the chestnuts are completely cooked.
4 Purée the soup in a food processor or blender until smooth, or put through a food mill. Season to taste with salt and pepper and serve hot, garnished with parsley.

Serves 4
Preparation time: 10 minutes, plus peeling the chestnuts
Cooking time: 45 minutes

CHESTNUT SOUP WITH PANCETTA AND ROSEMARY

1½ pounds fresh chestnuts or
2½ cups dried chestnuts, soaked overnight
in cold water
½ cup butter
5 ounces pancetta or regular bacon,
chopped
2 onions, finely chopped
1 carrot, chopped
1 celery stalk, chopped
1 tablespoon chopped rosemary
2 bay leaves
2 garlic cloves, halved
salt and black pepper

To garnish:
fresh rosemary sprigs

1 Peel the chestnuts according to the directions on page 9.
2 Melt the butter in a large pan and add the pancetta or bacon. Fry over medium heat until just starting to brown. Add the chopped onions, carrot, and celery, and cook for 5–10 minutes, or until they start to soften and brown.
3 Add the chestnuts to the pan, along with the chopped rosemary, bay leaves, and garlic. Add enough water to completely cover, and bring to a boil. Partially cover the pan, reduce the heat, and simmer for 30 minutes, stirring occasionally; the chestnuts should start to disintegrate and thicken the soup. Taste, and season well.
4 Ladle into warm bowls, garnish with rosemary sprigs, and serve.

Serves 6
Preparation time: 20 minutes, plus peeling the chestnuts
Cooking time: 1 hour

CHESTNUT AND PROSCIUTTO BITES

These tasty bites are quick and easy to prepare. Enjoy them as hot hors d'oeuvres,
or as canapés for a cocktail party.

12 thin slices of prosciutto
24 whole chestnuts, cooked and peeled
(see page 9)
Dijon mustard
freshly grated horseradish sauce (or, if
unavailable, bottled horseradish)
sun-dried tomato paste
mixed lettuce leaves, to garnish

1 Cut the pieces of prosciutto in half and on each slice, spread a small amount of mustard on one quarter, some horseradish on another quarter, and a bit of sun-dried tomato paste on the third quarter. Leave the last quarter plain.

2 Place a chestnut on each piece of the prepared prosciutto, and roll up tightly. Lightly grease a broiler pan, arrange the rolled-up bites on it, and broil for 4–5 minutes until hot. Let cool slightly before serving.

Serves 24
Preparation time: 15 minutes
Cooking time: 5 minutes

ROASTED CHESTNUTS

Serve roasted chestnuts as a pre-dinner snack to guests.
They should release a wonderful, toasted aroma when they are cooked.

1 pound chestnuts
1 tablespoon oil

1 Preheat the oven to 350°F.

2 Place a chestnut, flat side down, on a cutting board and hold it securely so that it doesn't wobble. Then, with a sharp paring knife, make two cuts in the shape of a cross on its shell, cutting down to the chestnut meat. Continue until all the chestnut shells have been slashed.

3 Heat a pan with an ovenproof handle over moderate heat. Add the oil, swirl to coat the bottom, and add the chestnuts. Shake until the chestnuts are sizzling, and remove from the burner.

4 Place in the preheated oven, and roast for about 30 minutes, at which point the shells and skins should come off easily.

Preparation time: 10 minutes
Cooking time: 35 minutes

CHESTNUT AND CRANBERRY SALAD WITH CITRUS DRESSING

This crunchy salad is delicious as an appetizer or snack, and also makes an excellent accompaniment
to cheese. Try it with a soft Brie and crusty bread. It is illustrated on page 3.

1 fennel bulb, thinly sliced
2 eating apples, cored and thinly sliced
2 celery stalks, sliced
½ cup cooked, peeled chestnuts, cut into small pieces
½ cup dried cranberries
grated lemon zest, to garnish

Citrus dressing:
1 tablespoon runny honey
juice and grated zest of 1 orange
1 tablespoon lemon juice
1 tablespoon olive oil
black pepper

1 Place the fennel, apples, celery, chestnuts, and cranberries in a large salad bowl.

2 To make the dressing, combine the honey, orange juice and zest, lemon juice, and oil in a bowl. Whisk lightly with a fork until it turns opaque. Season to taste with pepper. Pour the dressing over the salad ingredients and toss well. Serve immediately.

Serves 4
Preparation time: 25 minutes

CHESTNUT AND DUCK PATE

1 oven-ready duck
1½ pounds belly of pork, or other cut of
fat pork, ground
¼ pound bacon, ground
2 garlic cloves, crushed
1 teaspoon sea salt
10 black peppercorns
10 juniper berries, roughly crushed
1 cup cooked, peeled chestnuts
stock or water
2 tablespoons brandy
¾ cup red or white wine
bacon strips
melted lard, to cover (optional)
toast or bread, to serve

1 Preheat the oven to 375°F.

2 Prick the duck all over with a fork. Place on a rack over a roasting pan and cook the duck in the oven for 15 minutes, then remove and let cool. Trim the meat from the bones and chop it finely. Lower the oven heat to 350°F.

3 Mix the chopped duck with the ground meats and add the garlic, salt, peppercorns, and crushed juniper berries. Set aside for the flavors to develop while you prepare the chestnuts.

4 If using cooked chestnuts, skip this step. If using raw chestnuts, peel the chestnuts according to the directions on page 9. Put the peeled nuts in a small pan with enough stock or water to cover, and cook for about 8 minutes or until tender. Drain and cool.

5 Chop the chestnuts roughly and add to the meat mixture. Mix thoroughly and add the brandy and wine.

6 To check the seasoning, fry a tiny ball of the mixture in butter and taste it. It should be quite highly seasoned, so adjust the seasoning if necessary.

7 Line two ovenproof dishes (or molds) with the strips of bacon and divide the meat mixture between the two (or use a single ovenproof dish). Place the dishes in a baking pan half-filled with water, and bake, uncovered, in the preheated oven, for 1¼–1½ hours (plus 20 minutes longer if using a single dish). When ready, the pâtés will shrink away from the sides of the dishes.

8 Allow to cool for a couple of hours, then weight down with heavy can(s) to press out air pockets. Store the pâtés in the refrigerator, where they will keep for 1 week. To store for up to 1 month, pour melted lard over the tops to create an airtight seal, and refrigerate.

9 To serve, remove any lard used to seal, and turn the pâtés out on to serving dishes, leaving their jelly around them. Serve with toast or bread.

Serves 12–16 (6–8 per pâté)
Preparation time: 40 minutes, plus peeling the chestnuts and standing
Cooking time: 1¼–2 hours

CHESTNUT, GOAT CHEESE, AND RED ONION QUICHES

This recipe can also be made as one large quiche in a 10-inch pie dish. Adjust the quantities to 3 red onions,
6 sheets of phyllo dough, 2 goat cheese logs, ½ cup of milk and 3 eggs. Cook for 25–30 minutes. Serves 4–6.

1 red onion
2 tablespoons olive oil
12 sheets phyllo dough
½ cup butter, melted
1 cup cooked, peeled chestnuts
1 goat cheese log (about 5–7 ounces)
1 tablespoon chopped rosemary
1 tablespoon crushed, mixed peppercorns
⅓ cup milk
2 large eggs
1 tablespoon grated Parmesan cheese
salt

1 Preheat the oven to 325°F.

2 Peel and cut the onion into thin wedges, and spread them over the bottom of a roasting pan. Drizzle with the olive oil, and roast for about 30 minutes, or until softened.

3 Lightly grease four 4-inch individual pie dishes. Brush each sheet of phyllo dough with the melted butter, cut in half and line each dish with three buttered sheets.

4 Now layer the ingredients. Slice the chestnuts and cover the dough with them. Next, slice the goat cheese and arrange the slices over the chestnut layer. Spread the cooked onion on top of this, and sprinkle with the rosemary and crushed peppercorns.

5 To make the custard mixture, combine the milk and eggs in a bowl, whisk lightly, and season to taste with salt. Pour into the prepared pie dishes and sprinkle with the grated Parmesan. Place the pie dishes on a preheated baking sheet and bake for 20–25 minutes or until the custard mixture has set, and the edges of the pastry are golden brown. Serve hot or cold.

Serves 4
Preparation time: 50 minutes
Cooking time: 25 minutes

CHESTNUTS WITH BRUSSELS SPROUTS

1 pound Brussels sprouts
1⅓ cups cooked, peeled chestnuts
vegetable stock or water
2 tablespoons butter
salt and black pepper

1 Wash the Brussels sprouts in cold water, remove the outer leaves, and trim the ends. Place in a medium saucepan and cover with cold, lightly salted water. Bring slowly to a boil and cook, uncovered, for 5 minutes or until just tender. Drain well. Transfer to a warmed serving dish and keep warm.

2 While the sprouts are cooking, place the chestnuts in another saucepan, add enough vegetable stock or water to cover, and heat gently until warmed through.

3 Drain the chestnuts and stir into the sprouts, along with the butter. Season with salt and pepper, and serve hot.

Serves 4
Preparation time: 5 minutes
Cooking time: 10–12 minutes

CHESTNUTS WITH RED CABBAGE

1 pound chestnuts

1 cup prunes, soaked overnight, pitted and roughly chopped

1 cup peeled and chopped cooking apples

1 onion, chopped

2 pounds red cabbage, shredded

1 tablespoon sugar

2 tablespoons cider vinegar

1 cup beef stock

salt and black pepper

To garnish:
crispy, fried bacon, crumbled (optional)

1 Preheat the oven to 300°F.

2 Peel the chestnuts according to the directions on page 9, and cut the chestnuts in half.

3 In a casserole dish, layer the chestnuts, prunes, apples, onion, and red cabbage, and season with salt and pepper.

4 Mix together the sugar, vinegar, and stock, and pour over the vegetables.

5 Transfer the casserole to the oven, and cook for 2 hours, stirring occasionally. Taste, and if necessary, add a little more vinegar and sugar. Give it a stir, and serve, topped with bacon, if you like.

Serves 8–10

Preparation time: 10 minutes, plus peeling the chestnuts and soaking

Cooking time: 2 hours

WINTER MASHED POTATOES WITH CHESTNUTS

This makes a warming accompaniment to roast turkey, pork or goose. It is also a flexible dish,
so try adding turnips, rutabaga, or parsnips for a bit of variety.

2 large floury potatoes, such as russet
or Idaho, roughly chopped
I onion, roughly chopped
I ½ cups Brussels sprouts
2 cups cooked, peeled chestnuts
½ cup hot milk
¼ cup butter
salt and black pepper
rosemary sprig, pat of butter or chopped
chestnuts, to garnish

1 Place the potatoes and onion in a large pot of salted water and bring to a boil. Cook for 15 minutes, or until the potatoes are soft.
2 While the potatoes and onions are cooking, trim the Brussels sprouts, removing any wilted outer leaves, and cut them in half. Roughly chop the chestnuts. Once the potatoes are soft, add the sprouts and chestnuts to the pot. Cook for a further 5–6 minutes, or until the sprouts are soft.
3 Drain the vegetables and chestnuts and return them immediately to the pot. Sprinkle with salt and pepper to taste, and add the hot milk and butter. Mash everything together with a potato masher until thoroughly combined. Transfer to a warm serving dish and garnish with rosemary, butter or chopped chestnuts.

Serves 4
Preparation time: 10 minutes
Cooking time: 25 minutes

CHESTNUT AND BACON STUFFING

If you bake the stuffing on its own, serve it with gravy; the flavors blend nicely and will temper the sharpness of the citrus.

¼ pound bacon, chopped
3 celery stalks, finely chopped
I onion, finely chopped
I ¼ cups peeled, unsweetened chestnuts
(canned or from a jar), drained and finely
chopped or ⅔ cup dried chestnuts, soaked
in water overnight
4 cups fresh bread crumbs
juice and finely grated zest of I lemon
juice and finely grated zest of I orange
I egg, beaten
I tablespoon chopped fresh sage
salt and black pepper

1 Fry the bacon until browned. Add the celery and onion, and fry for about 5 minutes more, stirring occasionally.
2 In a large bowl, combine all the ingredients, along with the cooked bacon, celery, and onion, and mix together thoroughly.
3 Pack the stuffing loosely in the neck and body cavity of the bird. Alternatively, preheat an oven to 325°F and bake the stuffing in a greased, covered casserole dish for 30 minutes.

Makes 5 cups (enough to stuff a 10–12 pound bird)
Preparation time: about 20 minutes
Cooking time: 10 minutes if using as a stuffing in a bird or 30 minutes if baked separately

CHESTNUT AND SAUSAGE STUFFING

1 pound chestnuts or ¾ cup dried chestnuts,
soaked overnight
1 cup of milk
1 pound bulk pork sausage
1 tablespoon oil
4 cups fresh bread crumbs
4 medium shallots or 2 small, mild onions,
finely chopped
1 garlic clove, finely chopped
¼ cup finely chopped fresh parsley
1 tablespoon brandy
1 teaspoon sea salt
½–1 cup stock, to moisten (optional)
black pepper
ground mace or nutmeg

1 Peel the chestnuts according to the directions on page 9, or prepare the dried chestnuts according to the directions on page 9.
2 Simmer the chestnuts in the milk for 8–10 minutes until tender. Meanwhile, heat the oil in a frying pan and brown the sausage.
3 Drain the chestnuts, reserving the milk, and allow to cool. Chop the chestnuts coarsely and combine with the sausage in a bowl. Add the shallots or onions, garlic, parsley, brandy, sea salt, and season to taste with pepper and mace or nutmeg. Mix and add the reserved milk and/or stock until it reaches the consistency you like.
4 Pack the stuffing loosely in the neck and body cavity of a 10–12 pound bird. Alternatively, preheat an oven to 325°F and bake the stuffing in a greased, covered casserole dish for 30 minutes.

Makes 5 cups (enough to stuff a 10–12 pound bird)
Preparation time: 10–15 minutes, plus preparing the chestnuts
Cooking time: 10 minutes if using as a stuffing in a bird or 30 minutes if baked separately

CHESTNUT AND RAISIN STUFFING

1 pound chestnuts or ¾ cup dried
chestnuts, soaked overnight
4 cups fresh bread crumbs
2 tablespoons golden raisins
2 garlic cloves, crushed
4 celery stalks, finely chopped
3 tablespoons chopped fresh parsley
grated zest of ½ lemon
a little grated fresh ginger root
6 tablespoons sherry
½–1 cup stock, to moisten
salt and black pepper

1 Peel or prepare the chestnuts (see page 9).
2 In freshboiling water, cook the chestnuts gently for 20–30 minutes. Combine the prepared ingredients in a large bowl. Drain the chestnuts, reserving the cooking liquid. Mash the chestnuts with a fork, adding the reserved liquid if necessary. Scoop the mashed chestnuts into the bowl, mix well, and add some cooking liquid or stock to get the consistency you like.
3 Pack the stuffing loosely in the neck and body cavity of the bird. Alternatively, preheat an oven to 325°F and bake the stuffing in a greased, covered casserole dish for 30 minutes.

Makes 5 cups (enough to stuff a 10–12 pound bird)
Preparation time: 10–15 minutes, plus preparing the chestnuts
Cooking time: 20–30 minutes if using as a stuffing in a bird or 30 minutes if baked separately

CHESTNUT AND APPLE STUFFING

1 pound chestnuts or ¾ cup dried
chestnuts, soaked overnight
4 cups fresh bread crumbs
2 tablespoons chopped fresh parsley
1 large egg, beaten
½ pound belly pork, finely chopped
4 shallots or 2 small, mild onions, finely
chopped
1 pound eating apples, peeled, cored, and
chopped
½–1 cup stock, to moisten
salt and black pepper

1 Peel the chestnuts according to the directions on page 9, or prepare the dried chestnuts according to the directions on page 9.
2 Chop the chestnuts and mix with the bread crumbs, parsley, and egg in a large bowl. Season to taste with salt and pepper, set aside.
3 Cook the chopped pork in a skillet over medium heat until lightly browned (add a little oil if necessary). Add the shallots or onions, and cook until transparent. Then add the chopped apples and cook for about 5 minutes, stirring, until softened. Mix the cooked apples and pork mixture into the chestnut stuffing, and add enough stock to get the consistency you like.
4 Pack the stuffing loosely in the neck and body cavity of the bird. Alternatively, preheat an oven to 325°F and bake the stuffing in a greased, covered casserole dish for 30 minutes.

Makes 5–6 cups (enough to stuff a 10–12 pound bird)
Preparation time: 25 minutes, plus preparing the chestnuts
Cooking time: 10 minutes if using as a stuffing in a bird or 30 minutes if baked separately

CHESTNUT AND CRANBERRY STUFFING WITH FRESH HERBS

1 large onion, finely chopped
2 tablespoons vegetable oil
1 pound ground turkey or ground pork
1 cup fresh white bread crumbs
1 cup canned chestnuts, chopped
¼ cup dried cranberries
1 teaspoon chopped fresh thyme
2 teaspoons chopped fresh sage
1 egg, beaten
salt and black pepper

1 Preheat the oven to 400°F. Grease a 1-pound loaf pan.
2 In a skillet, heat the oil and lightly fry the onion until golden brown. Stir in the ground meat and bread crumbs and cook for 2–3 minutes. Add the chestnuts, cranberries, thyme, and sage. Mix together well and season to taste with salt and pepper.
3 Remove from the heat and stir in the beaten egg. Spoon into the prepared loaf pan and cook in the preheated oven for 1 hour, or until the top is a rich golden brown.
4 To serve, remove the stuffing from the pan and cut into 8 slices.

Serves 4
Preparation time: 10 minutes
Cooking time: about 1¼ hours

CHESTNUT AND POTATO PANCAKES WITH APPLE COMPOTE

Apple compote:
4 green eating apples, cored and diced
juice of I lemon
I tablespoon olive oil
I onion, thinly sliced
I tablespoon all-purpose flour
I cup flat dry (alcoholic) cider or ½ cup sweet apple cider plus ½ cup dry white wine
2 cups vegetable stock
2 tablespoons apple brandy or apple jack (optional)

Pancakes:
I pound floury potatoes, such as russet or Idaho
2 tablespoons all-purpose flour
I cup cooked, peeled chestnuts, sliced
I egg, beaten
¼ cup milk
salt and black pepper
butter, for frying

To garnish:
I cup thinly sliced Cheddar cheese
snipped chives

1 First make the compote. Place the prepared apples in a bowl, sprinkle with the lemon juice, toss, and set aside.

2 Heat the oil in a large skillet and fry the onion for 5–6 minutes until soft but not brown. Add the flour to the onion and stir well.

3 Stir in the cider and stock and let the mixture simmer gently, stirring constantly, until it has thickened. Add the apples, stir, and let the compote simmer over a gentle heat for about 25 minutes or until the apples are very soft and mushy. Finally stir in the apple brandy, if using. Set aside and keep warm.

4 To make the pancakes, cook the potatoes whole in boiling water for 10 minutes. Drain, and peel them while still warm. Grate them into a bowl, add the flour, and toss to combine. Add the chestnuts along with the egg and milk, and mix thoroughly. Season to taste with salt and pepper.

5 Heat a little butter in a frying pan and pour in a quarter of the pancake mixture. Cook the pancakes for 3–4 minutes on each side, until golden brown. Keep the pancakes warm as you cook the rest of the mixture.

6 To serve, place each pancake on a warm plate, spoon on some of the hot apple compote, and garnish with the Cheddar and some snipped chives.

Serves 4
Preparation time: 40 minutes
Cooking time: about 1½ hours

6/23/17
Wow!
Best. Risotto.
Ever

CHESTNUT, BACON, AND THYME RISOTTO

This recipe is illustrated on page 2.

3 tablespoons olive oil
1 onion, finely chopped
3 garlic cloves, finely chopped
4 strips bacon or prosciutto, diced
1 cup cooked, peeled chestnuts, roughly
chopped
2 cups Arborio rice
2 tablespoons fresh, chopped thyme
½ cup dry sherry or white wine
5 cups vegetable stock
¾ cup grated Parmesan cheese
salt and black pepper

To garnish:
grated Parmesan cheese
pat of butter (optional)

1 Heat the oil in a skillet. Add the onion and garlic, and fry for 3–4 minutes, until soft. Add the bacon or prosciutto and cook for a further 5–6 minutes, until the bacon is crisp and just starting to brown.

2 Add the chestnuts to the skillet, along with the rice. Cook for 1 minute, stirring constantly, until the rice is well coated with the oil. Stir in the thyme and sherry, and add 1 cup of the stock.

3 Reduce the heat until the risotto is on a slow simmer. Once the rice has absorbed the stock, add another cup of stock, and stir until that is absorbed. Continue to add the stock, 1 cup at a time, whenever the rice has absorbed the liquid. This will take about 30–35 minutes, at which point the rice should be soft and all the liquid absorbed.

4 Stir the grated Parmesan into the risotto and season to taste with salt and pepper. Transfer the hot risotto to a warm serving dish, and garnish with extra Parmesan, plus a pat of butter if you like. Serve with a green salad.

Serves 4
Preparation time: 15 minutes
Cooking time: 45 minutes

MIXED NUT ROAST

*This dish is cooked in a ring mold, but can also be baked in a large bread pan or individual loaf pans
or flan rings. It is excellent served hot or cold, and may be accompanied by a spicy tomato sauce.*

2 tablespoons olive or sunflower oil
I onion, finely chopped
I celery stalk, finely chopped
I garlic clove, finely chopped
2⅓ cups finely chopped mushrooms
I½ cups grated carrots
**I½ cups cooked, peeled chestnuts (canned
or vacuum-packed)**
**2 cups hazelnuts, walnuts, peanuts,
or pecans**
5 cups fine wholemeal fresh bread crumbs
I teaspoon grated lemon zest
I teaspoon finely chopped fresh marjoram
2 tablespoons finely chopped fresh parsley
I teaspoon ground mace
pinch of dried thyme
3 large eggs, beaten
⅔ cup vegetable stock or water
salt and black pepper

I Preheat the oven to 375°F. Lightly oil a 9½-inch ring mold.
Line carefully with plastic wrap, and smooth out any wrinkles.
Oil lightly.

2 Heat the oil in a large skillet and fry the onion, celery, and garlic
until soft. Add the mushrooms and fry until they color. Stir in the
carrots and cook for 5 minutes.

3 Meanwhile, combine all the nuts in a food processor and blend
until finely chopped but still having texture, or chop by hand.
Transfer to a large bowl and add the bread crumbs, lemon zest,
marjoram, parsley, mace, and thyme. Season to taste with salt
and pepper. Add the onion mixture, eggs, and stock or water, and
mix well.

4 Pack the mixture into the prepared mold, smooth out the top
making sure there are no air spaces, and cover with oiled foil. Set
the mold on a heavy baking sheet and place in the preheated oven.
Bake until firm to the touch; this will take about 1½ hours for the
mold, or 45 minutes if using two smaller containers.

5 When it is ready, remove the foil and carefully invert the nut
roast on to a warm serving dish. Remove the plastic wrap and
serve.

Makes about 30 slices
Preparation time: 30 minutes
Cooking time: 1–1¾ hours

ROAST TURKEY WITH STUFFING

For a different sized turkey, consult the label for the correct cooking time, and adjust the quantity of the stuffing accordingly, allowing ½ cup per pound of turkey. Any extra stuffing may be cooked in a greased, covered casserole dish in the oven for the last 30 minutes of roasting time. Allow 15–20 minutes per pound for turkeys weighing between 6–16 pounds, and add 5 minutes more per pound if the bird is stuffed.

10–12-pound oven-ready turkey, with
giblets removed
Chestnut and Bacon Stuffing or
see pages 24–25
¼ cup unsalted butter, melted
6–8 strips bacon
salt and pepper
holly sprigs, to garnish (optional)

For unstuffed turkey only:
1 apple, cored and quartered
1 onion, quartered

To serve:
cranberry sauce
gravy
selection of vegetables

1 Preheat the oven to 375°F.

2 Wash the inside of the turkey, dry thoroughly with paper towels, and season well with salt and pepper. If the turkey is to be cooked unstuffed, put the apple and onion quarters inside the body cavity. If the turkey is to be stuffed, pack the stuffing loosely into the neck and body cavity of the bird (but not too tightly or the heat will not penetrate the center of the bird). Truss the bird.

3 Place the turkey on a large sheet of strong foil and transfer to a roasting pan, large enough to just fit the bird. Brush the turkey with the butter, arrange the bacon strips over the breast and legs, and season well with salt and pepper. Insert a meat thermometer, if using, into the thickest part of the thigh, without touching the bone. Close the foil around the bird to make a loose parcel.

4 Roast in the preheated oven for 3–3¾ hours. Check the temperature at 2½ hours; if it's nearing 180°F, then open the foil and baste the turkey with its cooking juices. Leave the foil open to allow the bacon to become crisp and return it to the oven to cook for a further 30 minutes. The turkey is cooked when its internal temperature reaches 180°F; if cooking without a meat thermometer, pierce the thickest part of the thigh with a skewer or fork and when the juices run clear, it is done.

5 Carefully lift the turkey out of the pan, cover tightly with clean foil and set aside to rest in a warm place for 30 minutes.

6 Discard the trussing string. Transfer the turkey to a warmed serving platter, and garnish with holly sprigs, if using. Serve with cranberry jelly, gravy and a selection of vegetables.

Serves 8–10
Preparation time: about 15 minutes, plus resting
Cooking time: about 3–3¾ hours, depending on size and whether the bird is stuffed

CHESTNUT AND TURKEY CASSEROLE

2½ pounds boneless raw turkey meat, skinned and cubed
2 tablespoons vegetable oil
¼ cup butter
1 onion, sliced
1 garlic clove, chopped
1 cup button mushrooms
¼ cup plus 2 tablespoons all-purpose flour
⅔ cup turkey or chicken stock
2 tablespoons cranberry jelly
1½ cups cooked, peeled chestnuts
salt and black pepper
fresh parsley, to garnish
wild rice, to serve (optional)

Marinade:
2½ cups dry white wine
¼ cup white wine vinegar
1 onion, sliced
1 garlic clove, chopped
2 tablespoons fresh thyme
1 bay leaf
1 lemon slice
salt
12 black peppercorns, crushed

1 Combine all the marinade ingredients in a large bowl. Add the turkey and stir to coat thoroughly with the marinade. Cover and chill overnight.
2 Preheat the oven to 350°F.
3 Remove the turkey from the marinade and set aside. Strain the marinade and set that aside. Heat the oil in a large, heavy skillet and sauté the turkey until browned. Transfer the cooked turkey to a large flameproof casserole dish. (If you don't have a flameproof casserole dish, then use an ovenproof one, and use a skillet in Step 5, below.)
4 Melt the butter in the skillet, add the onion and garlic and cook, stirring, for 5 minutes. Add the mushrooms and cook a further 5 minutes. Sprinkle the flour into the pan and cook, stirring, for 2–3 minutes. Gradually whisk in the reserved marinade and stock and bring to a boil, stirring constantly. Remove from the heat, and stir in the cranberry jelly, salt, and pepper. Pour the sauce over the turkey pieces, cover, and cook in the preheated oven for 1 hour.
5 Transfer the turkey, mushrooms, and onions to a serving dish and keep warm. Place the flameproof casserole dish on the stove (or transfer the liquid from the casserole dish to the skillet), bring to a boil, and cook until it is reduced by a third. Add the chestnuts and simmer for 15 minutes. Coat the turkey with the sauce, and garnish with parsley. Serve with wild rice, if you like.

Serves 4
Preparation time: 40 minutes, plus marinating
Cooking time: 2 hours

HOT CHESTNUT AND CHICKEN SALAD

This salad makes a great light lunch or a light supper.

3 tablespoons olive oil
2 boneless, skinless chicken breasts, cut into strips
1 cup diced butternut squash
1 cup cooked, peeled chestnuts
1 teaspoon crushed, dried chiles
1 head romaine lettuce
1 handful arugula
1 small bunch flat-leaf parsley
1 zucchini, grated
salt and black pepper

1 Heat the oil in a skillet and add the chicken and the diced butternut squash. Cook for 8–10 minutes, until the chicken starts to brown and the squash is soft but still holds its shape.

2 Slice the chestnuts in half, and add them to the pan along with the chiles. Cook for a further 2–3 minutes, until the chestnuts are heated through. Season with salt and pepper, and set aside in a warm place.

3 Tear the lettuce leaves into pieces and place in a large serving bowl. Add the arugula and parsley leaves, along with the grated zucchini, and toss to mix. Just before serving, add the hot chicken and chestnut mixture and serve immediately.

Serves 4 as an appetizer, or 2 as a main course
Preparation time: 15 minutes
Cooking time: 15 minutes

RAVIOLI STUFFED WITH CHESTNUTS AND WILD MUSHROOMS

Rolling fresh herbs between the sheets of pasta has a pretty effect, but you can leave this out if you are short of time.
Any leftover pasta can be cut into long strips and either dried or frozen for later use.

3 large eggs
2½ cups semolina flour or all-purpose flour, plus extra for dusting
1 small bunch flat-leaf parsley
freshly grated Parmesan cheese, to serve

Filling:
1 cup dried wild mushrooms (porcinis or chanterelles)
1 cup cooked, peeled chestnuts
2 tablespoons olive oil
1 onion, finely chopped
2 garlic cloves, finely chopped
1 cup ricotta
pinch of nutmeg
salt and black pepper

Herbed butter:
1 cup butter
1 handful fresh sage leaves

1 Beat the eggs in a bowl and slowly add the pasta flour, adding just enough to form a firm dough. (Alternatively, combine the eggs and flour in an electric mixer, using the dough hook.) Cover the pasta dough with plastic wrap and let it rest for 1 hour.

2 To make the filling, put the dried mushrooms in a bowl, cover with cold water, and let soak for 30 minutes, then drain. Finely chop the mushrooms and chestnuts.

3 Heat the oil in a skillet, add the onion and garlic, and cook for 6–8 minutes, until soft but not brown.

4 In a large bowl, combine the chopped mushrooms, chestnuts, onion, garlic, and ricotta. Season to taste with nutmeg, and salt and pepper.

5 Divide the pasta into four pieces. You may use either a pasta machine, or roll the pasta out by hand using a rolling pin dusted with flour. Roll each piece out very thinly, to form a large rectangle. On two of the rectangles, stick the parsley leaves, using a little water. Cover these pieces with the other two pasta rectangles, press them down, and roll out again very thinly. Place small spoonfuls of the filling at intervals, two inches apart, on one of the pasta rectangles. Brush the spaces between the filling lightly with water. Cover with the remaining pasta sheet, and press down between the fillings. Cut the filled pasta into squares using a knife or crinkly cutter.

6 Bring a large pot of water to a boil, add the ravioli (in batches if necessary), and cook for about 3–4 minutes. Drain, and transfer to a warm pasta bowl.

7 While the ravioli is cooking, heat the butter in a pan and add the sage leaves. Fry for 1–2 minutes until the leaves are crisp. Pour the herbed butter over the ravioli and top with freshly grated Parmesan.

Serves 4
Preparation time: about 1 hour, plus resting and soaking
Cooking time: 15–20 minutes

PHEASANTS IN RED WINE WITH CHESTNUTS

4 oven-ready pheasants
3 tablespoons oil or drippings
2 large onions, sliced
2 tablespoons all-purpose flour
2 cups red wine
2 cups beef stock
1 tablespoon molasses
3–4 tablespoons brandy (optional)
1 bay leaf
14-ounce can whole peeled chestnuts, drained
salt and black pepper
parsley sprigs, to garnish

Stuffing balls:
¼ cup butter
2 onions, very finely chopped
1⅔ cups very finely chopped celery
2 tablespoons chopped fresh parsley
2 teaspoons fresh thyme
7 cups fresh white bread crumbs
2 eggs, beaten
a little lemon juice

1 Preheat the oven to 350°F.

2 Wipe the pheasants inside and out with paper towels, and season well with salt and pepper. Heat the oil in a large frying pan, add the pheasants one at a time and fry, turning, to brown all over. Transfer to a large roasting pan.

3 Add the onions to the frying pan and cook over a gentle heat for about 7 minutes, until lightly browned. Sprinkle in the flour and cook, stirring, for a further 1–2 minutes. Gradually stir in the wine and stock and bring to a boil. Add the molasses and brandy, if using, and stir to combine. Season well with salt and pepper, add the bay leaf, and simmer for 2 minutes.

4 Stir the chestnuts into the sauce, and then pour the sauce over the pheasants. Cover with foil, transfer to the preheated oven, and cook for about 1¼ hours, or until the pheasants are tender and thoroughly cooked.

5 Meanwhile, make the stuffing balls. Melt the butter in a frying pan, add the onions and celery, and fry over a gentle heat until soft. Transfer to a bowl, season with salt and pepper, and add the parsley and thyme. Add the bread crumbs and stir in the eggs to bind, with a little lemon juice. Form into 20 balls.

6 Arrange the stuffing balls on a greased baking sheet and cook with the pheasants for the last 30 minutes of cooking time.

7 Transfer the pheasants to a large warmed serving dish. Garnish with the stuffing balls and parsley sprigs. Discard the bay leaf from the pan and pour the the onion and chestnut sauce into heated gravy boats. Serve separately, with the carved pheasants.

Serves 10
Preparation time: about 40 minutes
Cooking time: about 1¾ hours

CHESTNUT, CELERY, AND MUSHROOM POT PIE

Filling:
2 tablespoons olive oil
I garlic clove, chopped
I onion, chopped
I carrot, chopped
3 celery stalks, chopped
14-ounce can chestnuts, drained and chopped
2⅓ cups chopped chestnut mushrooms
⅔ cup vegetable stock
⅔ cup ground almonds
I tablespoon chopped fresh parsley
2 eggs, beaten
salt and black pepper

Pastry dough:
3 cups all-purpose flour
I teaspoon salt
⅓ cup butter or margarine
¾ cup water
beaten egg, for glazing

I Preheat the oven to 400°F.
2 To make the filling, heat the oil in a frying pan, add the garlic and onion, and fry for about 5 minutes until softened. Add the carrot and celery and cook for 2–3 minutes more, stirring occasionally. Add the chestnuts, mushrooms, stock, almonds, and herbs, and stir. Season to taste with salt and pepper. Bring to a boil, stirring until the mixture is heated through and well combined. Remove from the heat, cool slightly, then stir in the eggs. Allow to cool.
3 To make the pastry dough, combine the flour and salt in a bowl. Melt the butter or margarine with the water in a saucepan. Add to the flour and mix quickly to form a soft dough. Wrap closely with plastic wrap and leave to rest at room temperature for 15 minutes.
4 Roll out two-thirds of the dough on a lightly floured surface and line a greased loaf pan (or deep pie dish or casserole dish) with it. Spread the chestnut mixture over the pie dough.
5 Roll out the remaining dough to a circle large enough to cover the pie. Dampen the edges of the pie lightly with water and cover with the rolled-out dough. Slide a knife along the sides to trim the excess dough, and reserve the trimmings. Pinch the edges of the pie to seal, and make a hole in the center to allow the steam to escape.
6 Roll out the dough trimmings and cut into leaves for decorations. Attach with a little of the beaten egg, then brush the top of the pie all over with the remaining egg to glaze.
7 Bake in the preheated oven for 40–50 minutes, or until the pastry is crisp and golden. Cool the pie for 10 minutes, then carefully remove the pie from its pan and serve.

Serves 6
Preparation time: 30 minutes, plus cooling and resting
Cooking time: about 1 hour

ROAST LOIN OF PORK
STUFFED WITH APRICOTS AND CHESTNUTS

*This dish is delicious served with roast butternut squash, especially if the sliced squash
is cooked in with the pork to absorb its juices.*

I large loin of pork (about 1¼ pounds)
3 tablespoons olive oil
3 tablespoons butter
salt and black pepper
flat-leaf parsley, to garnish

Stuffing:
¼ cup butter, softened
½ cup dried apricots, finely chopped
I cup cooked, peeled chestnuts, finely chopped
½ cup fresh bread crumbs
I large egg
⅛ cup chopped fresh parsley
½ teaspoon mild curry powder

I Preheat the oven to 325°F.

2 Make a deep incision into the loin of pork along its length, as deep as you can without cutting it in half. Cut along the sides also so that you can spread out the loin to make a large flat surface. Flatten the pork using a meat mallet and then season well with salt and pepper.

3 Place the olive oil and butter in a roasting pan and put it into the oven to heat up.

4 To make the stuffing, beat the butter in a bowl until it is creamy. Add the apricots and chestnuts to the butter with the bread crumbs, egg, parsley, and curry powder. Season to taste with salt and pepper and combine thoroughly. Spread the stuffing over the loin of pork and roll it up tightly lengthwise. Tie it with string to hold its shape, or pin it with fine metal skewers.

5 Remove the roasting pan from the oven and place the rolled pork in it. Roast the pork in the oven for about 30 minutes until golden brown, basting at intervals, and turning it over half way through. Serve the pork sliced, with its cooking juices and parsley to garnish. Roasted butternut squash or new potatoes are good accompaniments.

Serves 4
Preparation time: 20 minutes
Cooking time: 30 minutes

CHESTNUT TULIPS

Tulip baskets:
¼ cup plus 2 tablespoons all-purpose flour, sifted
¼ cup plus 2 tablespoons sugar
3 egg whites
2 tablespoons butter, melted
2 small oranges, for shaping
grated chocolate, to decorate (optional)

Chestnut cream:
4 ounces dark chocolate or 4 squares of semi-sweet baking chocolate, chopped
⅔ cup heavy cream
1 cup canned, unsweetened chestnut purée
1 tablespoon sugar
2 tablespoons brandy

1 Preheat the oven to 400°F.

2 Mix the flour and sugar in a bowl. Add the egg whites and butter, and beat until smooth. Place 3 tablespoons of the batter on a greased baking sheet and spread to form a 5-inch circle. Repeat with another 3 tablespoons of the batter.

3 Bake in the preheated oven for 4–5 minutes, until golden.

4 Let cool slightly, and while the circles cool, oil 2 small oranges. Remove the baked circles with a spatula and place each one, top side down, over the oranges, and mold them to create wavy edges. Leave these to set while you repeat the process with the remaining batter, making eight in all.

5 Gently heat the chocolate and cream in a pan. Once all the chocolate has melted, set the pan aside to cool.

6 Put the chestnut purée, sugar, chocolate mixture, and brandy in a blender or food processor until smooth. Pipe the mixture into the tulip cases and serve, decorated with some grated chocolate if you like.

Makes 8
Preparation time: 20–25 minutes
Cooking time: about 10 minutes

CHESTNUT ICE CREAM WITH CHOCOLATE SAUCE

This ice cream may be served simply scooped into individual bowls, or for an impressive dessert, molded and decorated. To mold the ice cream, pour the liquid mixture into a bread pan lined with aluminum foil, and freeze. To serve, unmold it, remove the foil, and decorate with whipped cream.

2 cups canned, unsweetened chestnut purée
¼ cup brandy
¾ cup sugar
2 cups heavy cream
2 egg whites
whipped cream, to serve (optional)

Chocolate sauce:
6 squares semi-sweet baking chocolate, chopped
⅔ cup water
½ cup sugar

1 Put the chestnut purée, brandy, and 2 tablespoons of the sugar in a bowl and beat until smooth. Whip the cream until it stands in soft peaks, then fold it into the chestnut mixture.

2 Beat the egg whites until stiff, then gradually beat in the remaining sugar. Continue beating until the mixture becomes very stiff, then fold it into the chestnut mixture. Scoop the ice cream into a rigid container and place in the freezer.

3 To make the chocolate sauce, put all the ingredients in a pan and heat very gently until the chocolate has melted and the sugar dissolves. Simmer, uncovered, for 10 minutes, then remove from the heat and leave to cool.

4 Transfer the ice cream to the refrigerator 20 minutes before serving to let soften. Scoop into individual bowls, pour the sauce over them, and decorate with whipped cream, if you like.

Serves 8
Preparation time: 40 minutes, plus freezing
Cooking time: 15 minutes

CHOCOLATE CHESTNUT TRUFFLES

Serve these rich, dark truffles with coffee after dinner,
or pack them into small boxes to give as presents to friends.

2 cups semi-sweet chocolate chips or
baking chocolate pieces
I cup unsweetened chestnut purée
¼ cup brandy
I teaspoon vanilla extract
½ cup heavy cream
cocoa powder, finely shredded Brazil nuts
or finely grated chocolate, for dusting

I Melt the chocolate in the top of a double boiler or in the microwave. Place the chestnut purée in a bowl and mix in the brandy, vanilla extract, and cream.

2 Add the melted chocolate to the bowl and mix everything thoroughly. Let the mixture cool until it is dense enough to roll into balls.

3 Roll the mixture into walnut-sized balls and dust them with the cocoa powder, finely shredded nuts, or grated chocolate. The truffles will keep in the refrigerator for up to a week.

Makes about 24 truffles
Preparation time: 45 minutes, plus cooling
Cooking time: about 3 minutes

MARRON MERINGUES

The meringues on their own will keep for up to 10 days if stored in an airtight container, but once they have been assembled with the chestnut filling, they should be chilled and served within 2–3 hours.

Meringues:
⅓ cup light brown sugar
⅓ cup sugar
3 egg whites

Filling:
1 cup sweetened chestnut purée
1 tablespoon rum or coffee liqueur
⅔ cup heavy cream

1 Preheat the oven to 225°F. Cover 2 cookie sheets with baking parchment or wax paper.

2 Sift the two sugars together until evenly blended.

3 Beat the egg whites in a bowl until very stiff and standing in peaks. Beat in the sugar mixture, 1 tablespoon at a time, until thoroughly incorporated; once the meringue is stiff again, add more sugar. For the last third of the sugar, either beat it in or fold it in, whichever you prefer.

4 Put the meringue into a pastry bag fitted with a large star-shaped decorating nozzle. Squeeze the meringue out into 4-inch bar-shaped lengths on to the prepared cookie sheets, until all the meringue is used up.

5 Bake in the preheated oven for 2 hours. The meringues should then be set. To check, see if one will peel easily off the paper; if not, cook for a further 15 minutes and try again. When ready, slide the paper and meringues on to a cooling rack, and let cool.

6 Once the meringues are cool, remove from the paper and store in an airtight container until needed.

7 To make the filling, combine the chestnut purée and rum or liqueur, and beat until smooth. In a separate bowl, whip the cream until stiff and fold it into the chestnut mixture.

8 To assemble, sandwich the meringues together, with the chestnut filling in the middle, and chill. Serve within 2–3 hours.

Makes 12
Preparation time: about 30 minutes
Cooking time: 2–2¼ hours

CHESTNUT MERINGUE NESTS

Meringue:
3 egg whites
I cup sugar

Filling:
I cup canned, sweetened chestnut purée
I tablespoon sugar
2 tablespoons brandy
⅔ cup heavy whipping cream, whipped

To decorate: (optional)
8 rose leaves
dark chocolate, melted

1 Preheat the oven to 275°F.

2 Beat the egg whites until stiff, then gradually beat in the sugar.

3 Line a cookie sheet with baking parchment or wax paper. Fill a pastry bag, fitted with a large fluted nozzle, with the meringue, and squeeze out eight 3-inch circles. Then pipe the meringue around the edge of each circle to form a nest. Clean the pastry bag and nozzle for Step 5, below.

4 Bake in the preheated oven for 1½ hours, at which point the meringues should be set. To check, see if one will peel easily off the paper; if not, cook for a further 15 minutes and try again. When ready, slide the paper and meringues on to a cooling rack, and let cool.

5 To make the filling, beat the chestnut purée with the sugar and brandy until blended, then fold in the whipped cream. Fill the pastry bag, fitted with the large fluted nozzle, with the chestnut mixture and squeeze it into the nests.

6 To make the chocolate rose leaves, if using, coat the underside of each leaf with the melted chocolate, using a fine paint brush. Leave them, chocolate side up, until set. Then carefully lift the tip of the leaf, and peel it away from the chocolate.

7 Decorate each nest with a chocolate rose leaf, and serve.

Serves 8
Preparation time: 45 minutes
Cooking time: 1½–1¾ hours

CHESTNUT FLORENTINES

¾ **cup unsalted butter**
¾ **cup light brown sugar**
3 tablespoons heavy cream
⅓ **cup all-purpose flour**
1 cup cooked, peeled chestnuts
1 cup sliced almonds
½ **cup raisins**
about 4 ounces white or semi-sweet chocolate, for coating

1 Preheat the oven to 350°F. Grease two baking sheets.

2 Melt the butter in a pan. Stir in the sugar and let the mixture come to a boil, stirring occasionally. Add the cream and stir, until fully blended. Blend in the flour and let the mixture cook for 2 minutes. Remove from heat and set aside.

3 Finely chop the chestnuts and add them to the mixture, along with the almonds and raisins, and combine thoroughly. Drop spoonfuls of the florentine mixture on to the greased tray, spacing them at least an inch apart to allow for spreading.

4 Bake the florentines in the preheated oven for 7–10 minutes, until they start to brown at the edges. Remove the tray from the oven and, using a metal spoon, gently push in the edges of the florentines to make them round. Return them to the oven for another 3–4 minutes, until they are golden brown. Let cool until they are set, then lift them gently and place on a cooling rack.

5 When the florentines are cold, melt the chocolate and dip the edges of the florentines into it, or else drizzle the melted chocolate over the tops of them. Leave the chocolate to set before serving the cookies. They are great served with coffee.

Makes 18
Preparation time: 20 minutes
Cooking time: 15–20 minutes

CHESTNUT MOUSSE

2 eggs, separated
⅔ cup milk
2 teaspoons granulated gelatin
2 tablespoons water
I cup canned, sweetened, chestnut purée
⅔ cup heavy cream

To decorate:
⅓ cup heavy cream, whipped

I In the bottom of a double boiler, heat some water to barely simmering, but do not boil. Put the egg yolks and milk in the top of the double boiler and stir constantly, until the custard thickens and coats the back of a spoon. Remove the double boiler from the heat and set aside.

2 In a small pan, dissolve the gelatin in the 2 tablespoons of water over a gentle heat. Beat the gelatin into the chestnut purée, along with the custard. Cool slightly, then add the heavy cream.

3 Beat the egg whites until stiff, then lightly fold into the chestnut mixture. Spoon the mousse into 4 individual serving dishes and chill until set.

4 Top each one with a spoonful of the whipped cream, and serve.

Serves 4
Preparation time: 15 minutes, plus chilling
Cooking time: 10–15 minutes

ITALIAN CHESTNUT PUREE WITH CREAM

I pound chestnuts
2 tablespoons fresh orange juice
1½ cups confectioners' sugar, sifted
pinch of salt

Topping:
⅔ cup heavy cream
2 tablespoons brandy or rum

I Peel the chestnuts according to the directions on page 9.

2 Place the chestnuts in a pan, cover with cold water, and bring to a boil. Simmer for 45 minutes or until soft. Drain the chestnuts, and purée them with the orange juice in a food processor or blender, or mash together with a fork. Stir in the sugar and salt.

3 Spoon the purée into individual serving dishes. Whip the cream with the brandy or rum until thick but not stiff. Swirl lightly over the top of each portion, and serve.

Serves 4
Preparation time: 20 minutes, plus peeling the chestnuts
Cooking time: 1 hour

MONTE BIANCO

The origins of this dessert are obscure, apart from the fact that it takes its name from Mont Blanc in the French Alps. In Italy, cooks make Monte Bianco on special occasions.

three 8-ounce cans chestnuts, drained
¼ cup rum
½ cup water
¼ cup sugar
2 tablespoons fennel seeds
1 cup heavy cream
2 tablespoons confectioners' sugar

1 Put the chestnuts and rum in a food processor or blender and blend until puréed. Transfer the purée to a bowl.

2 Put the water, sugar, and fennel seeds in a small heavy saucepan and heat gently until the sugar has dissolved. Increase the heat and boil the liquid for about 5 minutes, until reduced and syrupy. Strain the syrup into the purée and beat well to mix, then taste, and beat in more rum and sugar if you like.

3 Form the purée into a single cone shape on a serving plate, and chill in the refrigerator for 1–2 hours.

4 Whip the cream and confectioners' sugar until the cream holds its shape. Then swirl it all over the chestnut mound, as if you were frosting a cake. Chill in the refrigerator until serving time.

Serves 6
Preparation time: 30 minutes, plus chilling
Cooking time: 10 minutes

CHESTNUT CREME BRULEES

These brûlées are topped with a light, crunchy layer of caramel, but you can make them in the traditional way by coating them with sugar and placing them under a hot broiler until the sugar has caramelized. These can be made a day in advance and kept in the refrigerator. Top with the caramel just before serving.

2 cups heavy cream
1 vanilla bean
6 egg yolks
⅓ cup light brown sugar
2 tablespoons dark rum
1 cup cooked, peeled chestnuts

Caramel:
1 cup sugar
¼ cup water

1 Preheat the oven to 300°F.

2 Pour the cream into a saucepan. Split the vanilla bean along its length and scrape the seeds into the cream; add the vanilla bean also. Heat the cream until just below boiling point and then remove the pan from the heat. Leave to stand for 15 minutes then discard the bean.

3 Finely chop the chestnuts and divide them among 6 ramekins.

4 Beat the egg yolks in a bowl, along with the sugar and rum. Add the cream and mix well. Fill the ramekins the rest of the way with the cream and egg yolk mixture.

5 Place the ramekins in a deep roasting pan. Fill the pan with cold water, being careful not to let any fall into the brûlées, and stop pouring when the water reaches three-quarters of the way up the sides of the ramekins. Place the pan in the preheated oven and cook the custards for about 30–35 minutes, until they have set. It is important that they do not overcook or rise, because the mixture will separate.

6 Remove the ramekins from the roasting pan using a cloth or potholders, and allow them to cool. Once they have cooled, place them in the refrigerator until ready to add their topping.

7 To make the caramel topping, combine the sugar and water in a pan and place over medium heat, stirring until the sugar has dissolved. Let the mixture boil gently until it turns golden brown—do not stir it again or it will crystallize. Drizzle the caramel over the chilled brûlées and return them to the refrigerator until ready to serve. (Note: Once they have been topped with the caramel, the brûlées should be eaten within a few hours, otherwise the caramel will start to dissolve.)

Makes 6
Preparation time: 20 minutes, plus chilling
Cooking time: 35–40 minutes

FRENCH CHRISTMAS PUDDING

2 cups unsweetened chestnut purée
½ cup unsalted butter, softened
4 eggs, separated
¾ cup sugar
2 tablespoons brandy (optional)

Chocolate sauce:
⅔ cup heavy cream
8 squares semi-sweet baking chocolate,
broken into pieces
2 tablespoons brandy

To decorate:
4 marrons glacés, sliced

1 Preheat the oven to 350°F. Grease and line a 1-quart loaf pan.
2 Cream the chestnut purée and butter, then beat in the egg yolks, sugar, and brandy, if using. Beat the egg whites until stiff and fold them into the chestnut mixture, then pour into the prepared pan. Place the loaf pan in a roasting pan which has been half-filled with water, and bake for 2 hours, until set. Cover with a piece of buttered aluminium foil, if necessary during cooking.
3 Meanwhile, prepare the sauce. Heat the cream in a small heavy pan over a gentle heat; do not let it boil. Add the chocolate and brandy and stir, until the chocolate has melted and the sauce is smooth. Set aside.
4 Remove the pudding from the oven, lift it out of the water-bath, and let it cool for 5–10 minutes. Loosen the sides with a knife and unmold it on to a warmed platter. Coat with a little chocolate sauce, decorate with the marrons glacés, and serve. Pour the remaining sauce into a gravy boat or other suitable container, and let people pour on their own.

Serves 8
Preparation time: 30 minutes
Cooking time: 2 hours

PANETTONE WITH CHESTNUTS

This delicious Italian cake is yeast-based, which means you'll have to wait
for it to rise before baking, but it's well worth the wait.

3½ cups all-purpose flour
1 packet fast-action dried yeast
⅓ cup sugar
pinch of salt
½ cup lukewarm milk
½ cup melted butter
2 eggs
grated zest of 1 lemon
few drops of vanilla extract
½ teaspoon ground nutmeg
½ cup chopped citron
½ cup raisins
1 cup cooked, peeled chestnuts, chopped

To glaze:
1 egg, beaten
¼ cup rock sugar, or crushed white sugar cubes

1 Preheat the oven to 350°F. Line the bottom of a deep, 7-inch cake pan with wax paper, and grease the sides.

2 Mix the flour, yeast, sugar, and salt in a large bowl. Add the milk, butter, eggs, lemon zest, vanilla, and nutmeg, and mix well to form a soft dough. Turn the dough out onto a lightly floured surface and knead it for 10 minutes. (Alternatively, knead the dough using an electric mixer fitted with a dough hook.) Place the dough back in the bowl, cover with a damp cloth, and leave in a warm place to rise for about 1 hour or until doubled in bulk.

3 Place the dough on a lightly floured surface and knead into it the chopped citron, raisins, and chestnuts. Roll the dough into a ball and place it in the prepared cake pan. Cover it again with the damp cloth and let it stand for about 20 minutes or until it reaches the top of the pan.

4 Brush the top of the panettone with the beaten egg and sprinkle the sugar over it. Bake in the preheated oven for 35–40 minutes, until the top is golden brown. Turn it out of the pan and let it cool on a wire rack. Once cooled, slice and serve.

Makes one 7-inch cake
Preparation time: 25 minutes, plus rising
Cooking time: 35–40 minutes

CREPES FILLED WITH CHESTNUT CREAM AND AMARETTO

Any liqueur may be used in this recipe; try experimenting with Cointreau, Drambuie, or brandy.

Crêpes:
I cup all-purpose flour
I large egg
I cup milk
I tablespoon vegetable oil

Chestnut cream:
I cup unsweetened chestnut purée
grated zest of I orange, plus extra to decorate
2 tablespoons Amaretto di Saronno
2 tablespoons sugar
I cup heavy cream

Syrup:
I cup maple syrup
½ cup finely chopped, cooked chestnuts
2 tablespoons Amaretto di Saronno

I Sift the flour into a bowl and gradually whisk in the egg and milk. Stir in the oil and let the batter rest for 30 minutes.

2 To make the chestnut cream, put the chestnut purée in a bowl with the orange zest, Amaretto, and sugar, and mix to combine. In another bowl, whip the cream until it forms soft peaks. Fold the cream into the purée mixture and refrigerate until needed.

3 To cook the crêpes, lightly brush a medium-sized non-stick frying pan with oil, and heat it over a medium heat. Drop in a couple of tablespoonfuls of the batter and swirl it around the pan until it evenly coats the bottom. Cook each crêpe for about 1–2 minutes on each side, until golden brown. As you cook them, keep the cooked crêpes warm in the oven, covered in foil.

4 To make the syrup, heat the maple syrup and chopped chestnuts in a pan, bring to a boil, and stir in the Amaretto. Remove the warm crêpes from the oven, and the chestnut cream from the refrigerator. Fill each crêpe with the chestnut cream, roll it up, and arrange on individual plates or a warm serving platter. Drizzle the heated syrup over the crêpes, and serve immediately decorated with grated orange zest.

Makes 8 (to serve 4)
Preparation time: 10 minutes, plus resting
Cooking time: 25–40 minutes

CHESTNUT AND CHOCOLATE ROULADE

3 eggs, separated
½ cup sugar
4 ounces dark chocolate or 4 squares
semi-sweet baking chocolate, broken into
pieces
2 tablespoons water
2 cups unsweetened chestnut purée
sifted confectioners' sugar, for sprinkling

To finish:
2 tablespoons honey
2 tablespoons Grand Marnier
⅔ cup heavy cream, whipped

1 Preheat the oven to 350°F. Grease an 8 x 12-inch jellyroll pan and line it with wax paper.

2 Beat the egg yolks and sugar until thick and creamy.

3 Heat the chocolate and water in the top of a simmering double boiler, and stir until melted. Remove from the heat and mix in half of the chestnut purée, then gradually beat in the egg yolk mixture. In a separate bowl, beat the egg whites until fairly stiff, then fold them into the chocolate mixture.

4 Scrape the batter into the prepared jellyroll pan, place in the preheated oven, and bake for 25–30 minutes, or until a toothpick comes out clean. Allow to cool, then cover with a clean damp cloth and leave in the refrigerator overnight.

5 The next day, sift some confectioners' sugar on to a sheet of wax paper. Remove the cake from the refrigerator and carefully lift off the cloth. Lay the cake on the sugared wax paper, and peel off the lining paper.

6 Beat the remaining chestnut purée with the honey and liqueur, then whisk into the whipped cream. Spread the cream mixture over the roulade and roll up like a jellyroll. Sprinkle thickly with confectioners' sugar, and serve.

Serves 8
Preparation time: 30 minutes, plus chilling
Cooking time: 30–35 minutes

CHOCOLATE AND CHESTNUT CAKE

2¼ cups cooked, peeled chestnuts
3 ounces dark chocolate or
3 squares semi-sweet baking chocolate,
broken into pieces
2 tablespoons water
4 eggs, separated
1 cup sugar

To decorate:
1¼ cups heavy cream, whipped
1 marron glacé, cut into pieces

1 Preheat the oven to 350°F. Line the bottoms of two 8-inch round cake pans with wax paper, and grease the sides.
2 Purée the chestnuts in a food processor or blender until fairly smooth; add a little water if necessary. Scoop into a large bowl.
3 Place the chocolate and water in the top of a simmering double boiler, and stir until smooth and melted. Add the egg yolks and sugar and whisk until thick enough to leave a trail. Pour the chocolate sauce into the puréed chestnuts, and mix well. In a separate bowl, beat the egg whites until stiff, then fold into the chestnut batter.
4 Pour the batter into the prepared cake pans, place in the preheated oven, and bake for 35–40 minutes. Leave in the pans to cool, then ease the cakes out of the pans onto a cooling rack and allow to cool completely.
5 When the cakes have cooled, use half the whipped cream to sandwich them together. Spread more cream over the top of the cake. Using a pastry bag fitted with a rosette nozzle, pipe some rosettes on top of that if you like. Decorate with the pieces of marron glacé and chill until ready to serve.

Makes one 8-inch cake
Preparation time: 45 minutes, plus cooling
Cooking time: 40–45 minutes

BUCHE DE NOEL

This cake dates from 1870 and was made by Parisian pastry cooks. Inspired by the real log which used to burn in the hearth throughout Christmas, Bûche de Noël is often called a "Yule Log."

4 eggs
½ cup sugar, plus extra for dredging
½ cup, plus 2 tablespoons all-purpose flour
1 tablespoon cocoa powder
2 tablespoons butter, melted and cooled

Filling:
⅔ cup heavy cream
1 tablespoon milk
1 cup canned sweetened chestnut purée
or ⅔ cup unsweetened chestnut purée
blended with 2 tablespoons sugar

Crème au beurre au chocolat:
⅓ cup sugar
¼ cup water
2 egg yolks
½–¾ cup unsalted butter
2 squares semi-sweet baking chocolate,
broken into pieces

To decorate:
confectioners' sugar
cocoa powder, sifted
holly leaves

1 Heat the oven to 375°F. Line a 12 x 10-inch jellyroll pan with greased wax paper.

2 Put the eggs and sugar in a bowl and beat until the mixture is thick and pale, and the beater leaves a heavy trail when lifted. Sift the flour and cocoa together twice and fold into the mixture, followed by the cooled butter. Spread the batter in the prepared pan, spreading it right out to the corners. Bake in the oven for 15–20 minutes, until just firm and springy to the touch.

3 Unmold onto a sheet of wax paper covered with sugar. Peel the paper from the cake and trim the edges with a sharp knife. Roll up the cake with the sugared paper inside and cool on a wire rack.

4 To make the filling, whip the cream and milk together until stiff, then fold the mixture into the chestnut purée. Unroll the cake carefully, remove the paper, and spread it evenly with the filling. Re-roll carefully and set aside.

5 To make the crème au beurre, put the egg yolks in a bowl, and have your beaters ready. Combine the sugar and water in a heavy-based pan and heat gently until dissolved. Bring to a boil and boil steadily for 3–4 minutes until it reaches 225°F, or until the syrup forms a thin thread. With your beaters running, pour the syrup in a thin stream on to the egg yolks. Continue to beat until the mixture is thick and cold. In a separate bowl, beat the butter until soft, then gradually beat it into the egg mixture. Place the chocolate with 1 tablespoon water in the top of a simmering double boiler, and stir continuously until smooth and melted. Cool slightly, then beat the chocolate into the egg mixture.

6 Coat the cake with the chocolate mixture; then mark with a butter knife to make it look like tree bark. Chill until set. Dust lightly with cocoa powder and confectioners' sugar, and decorate with holly leaves to serve.

Serves 8
Preparation time: 45 minutes, plus chilling
Cooking time: 25–30 minutes

MARRONS GLACES

2 pounds fresh chestnuts
a few drops of vanilla extract

First syrup:
2 cups sugar
I cup water
I pinch cream of tartar

Second syrup:
2 cups sugar
¼ cup water
I pinch cream of tartar
a few drops of vanilla extract

1 Peel the chestnuts according to the directions on page 9, making sure the nuts are completely free of any pieces of skin.

2 Put the chestnuts into a pot of fresh water, along with a few drops of vanilla, and bring to a boil. Continue boiling for about 15 minutes, until tender, and then drain and set aside.

3 To make the first syrup, combine the sugar, water, and cream of tartar in a saucepan and bring to a boil. Continue boiling until the syrup reaches 220°F on a sugar thermometer; this will be quite a thin syrup. Add the chestnuts to the syrup, boil for a further minute, then remove from heat. Let the chestnuts soak in the syrup for 48 hours, then drain them and set aside. Discard the syrup.

4 To make the second syrup, combine the sugar, water, and cream of tartar in a saucepan and stir until the sugar dissolves. Bring to a boil and continue boiling until the syrup reaches 250°F on a sugar thermometer, or the "firm ball" stage. (The "firm ball" stage has been reached once you can form a firm but pliable ball from a drop of sugar syrup that has been dropped into cold water.) Add vanilla to taste, and drop in the chestnuts. Remove from the heat and stir the chestnuts until well coated.

5 Using a slotted spoon, lift out the chestnuts and arrange on a wire rack. Leave to dry for a couple of days before serving.

Makes 2 pounds
Preparation time: about 25 minutes over 5–6 days
Cooking time: 30–40 minutes

Chestnut Jam with Whiskey

This jam is delicious simply spread on toast, but should
also be tried layered with cream or yogurt, as a dessert.

1¼ pounds cooked, peeled chestnuts
1 vanilla bean
1¾ cups light brown sugar
2 tablespoons whiskey

1 Sterilize a large jam jar by immersing it in a pot of water and bringing the water to a light boil. Let it simmer gently for 10 minutes. You may leave the jar in the hot water until shortly before you will need it, then remove it with tongs and let it air-dry on a rack.

2 Place the chestnuts and vanilla bean in a heavy pot and add enough water just to cover them. Bring to a boil and simmer for 30 minutes. Remove the vanilla bean, and strain and reserve the cooking liquid. Purée the chestnuts in a food processor or blender, adding a little of the reserved liquid if necessary, or put them through a food mill.

3 Put the chestnut purée back in the pan. Slice the vanilla bean lengthways and scrape the seeds into the pan. Add the sugar and a ½ cup of the cooking liquid and stir to blend. Bring to a boil, stirring frequently, and cook for about 5 minutes or until very thick. Remove from the heat and add the whiskey.

4 Spoon the warm jam into the sterilized jar and bang the jar on the counter to remove any air bubbles. Place a square of wax paper over the top of the jam. Screw the lid on tightly and leave for a couple of days in a cool place before opening. The jam will keep for up to 6 months, unopened, if stored in a cool, dry place. Refrigerate after opening.

Makes ½ pint
Preparation time: 15 minutes, plus peeling the chestnuts and sterilizing the jar
Cooking time: about 45 minutes

CHESTNUT, RED ONION, AND FENNEL CHUTNEY

This chutney is the perfect partner to blue cheese, bread and cold cuts.

¼ cup olive oil
4 large red onions, thinly sliced
1 fennel bulb, trimmed and thinly sliced
2 cups cooked, peeled chestnuts
½ cup light brown sugar
½ cup cider vinegar
⅓ cup sherry
black pepper

1 Sterilize a large jam jar (see page 61).
2 Heat the oil in a large skillet, add the onions and fennel, and cook gently for 25–30 minutes, until the onions are very soft.
3 Cut the chestnuts in half and add them to the pan, along with the sugar, vinegar, and sherry. Season well with pepper and stir. Let the mixture simmer gently, stirring occasionally, for about 1 hour, until the liquid has thickened.
4 Spoon the chutney into the sterilized jar and screw the lid on tightly. Let the chutney cool completely before serving. Store in a cool, dry place or in the refrigerator. It will keep for 3–4 months.

Makes 1 pint
Preparation time: 15 minutes
Cooking time: 1½ hours

INDEX

A

apples: chestnut and
apple soup 12
chestnut and apple
stuffing 25
chestnut and potato
pancakes with apple
compote 26
apricots: roast loin of
pork stuffed with
chestnuts and 38

B

bacon: chestnut and
bacon stuffing 22
chestnut, bacon and
thyme risotto 28
boiled chestnuts 10
braised chestnuts 10
Brussels sprouts,
chestnuts with 20
buche de Noël 58

C

cakes: buche de Noël 58
chocolate and
chestnut cake 57
canned chestnuts 9
celery, chestnut and
mushroom pot pie 37
cheese: chestnut, goat
cheese and red onion
quiches 18
chestnut cream 9
chestnut purée 9, 10
chicken: hot chestnut
and chicken salad 33
chocolate: buche de
Noël 58

chestnut and
chocolate roulade 56
chestnut Florentines
46
chestnut ice cream
with chocolate sauce
41
chestnut tulips 40
chocolate and
chestnut cake 57
chocolate chestnut
truffles 42
French Christmas
pudding 52
Christmas pudding,
French 52
chutney, chestnut, red
onion and fennel 62
cranberries: chestnut
and cranberry salad
16
chestnut and
cranberry stuffing 25
cream of chestnut soup
12
crème brûlées, chestnut
50
crêpes filled with
chestnut cream and
Amaretto 54

D

dried chestnuts 9
duck and chestnut pâté
17

F

fennel, chestnut and red
onion chutney 62
Florentines, chestnut 46
flour, chestnut 9, 10

French Christmas
pudding 52

I

ice cream, chestnut 41
Italian chestnut purée
48

J

jam, chestnut with
whiskey 61

M

marron meringues 44
marrons glacés 6, 9, 60
meringues: chestnut
meringue nests 45
marron meringues 44
Monte Bianco 49
mousse, chestnut 48
mushrooms: chestnut,
celery and mushroom
pot pie 37
mixed nut roast 29
ravioli stuffed with
wild mushrooms 34

N

nut roast 29

O

onions: chestnut, goat
cheese and red onion
quiches 18
chestnut, red onion
and fennel chutney
62

P

pancakes: chestnut and
potato pancakes 26

crêpes filled with
chestnut cream and
Amaretto 54
pancetta, chestnut soup
with rosemary and 13
panettone with
chestnuts 53
pâté, chestnut and duck
17
peeling chestnuts 9-10
pheasants in red wine
with chestnuts 36
pies: chestnut, celery
and mushroom pot
pie 37
pork: roast loin of pork
stuffed with apricots
and chestnuts 38
potatoes: chestnut and
potato pancakes 26
winter mashed
potatoes with
chestnuts 22
preserve, basic chestnut
10
prosciutto and chestnut
bites 14

Q

quiches, chestnut, goat
cheese and red onion
18

R

raisin and chestnut
stuffing 24
ravioli stuffed with
chestnuts and wild
mushrooms 34
red cabbage, chestnuts
with 21

risotto, chestnut, bacon
and thyme 28
roast turkey with
stuffing 30
roasted chestnuts 16
roulade, chestnut and
chocolate 56

S

salads: chestnut and
cranberry 16
hot chestnut and
chicken 33
sausage and chestnut
stuffing 24
soups 12-13
stuffings: apricots and
chestnuts 38
chestnut and apple 25
chestnut and bacon 22
chestnut and
cranberry 25
chestnut and raisin 24
chestnut and sausage
24

T

truffles, chocolate
chestnut 42
tulips, chestnut 40
turkey: chestnut and
turkey casserole 32
roast turkey with
stuffing 30

V

vacuum packed
chestnuts 9